Big Ears

Written by Jo Windsor

Rigby

The fox has
big ears.

ears

ears

The bat has
big ears.

The goat has
big ears.

ears

The dog has
big ears.

ears

The rabbit has
big ears.

ears

The elephant has big ears.

ears

Index

▬▬ Guide Notes

Title: Big Ears

Stage: Emergent – Magenta

Genre: Nonfiction (Expository)

Approach: Guided Reading

Processes: Thinking Critically, Exploring Language, Processing Information

Written and Visual Focus: Photographs (static images), Index, Labels

Word Count: 30

FORMING THE FOUNDATION

Tell the children that this book is about the big ears that some animals have.
Talk to them about what is on the front cover. Read the title and the author.
Focus the children's attention on the index and talk about the different ears
in the book.
"Walk" through the book, focusing on the photographs and talk about the different
ears, e.g., shape, place on the body.

Read the text together.

THINKING CRITICALLY
(sample questions)

After the reading
• What is the same about some of the animals' ears and what is different?
• Why do you think the ears have to be where they are on the animals' body?

EXPLORING LANGUAGE
(ideas for selection)

Terminology
Title, cover, author, photographs

Vocabulary
Interest words: fox, ears, bat, goat, dog, rabbit, elephant
High-frequency words: the, has